1498

1498

AMERICA

SMITHMARK

Text
Patrizia Raffin

Translation
Richard Reville

Graphic design
Patrizia Balocco

Contents

A Country without Frontiers......................*page 32*
Metropolises ....*page 64*
A Style of Life..*page 96*

2-3 *One of the most spectacular spots in Utah, which in terms of natural wonders is second to no other state in the U.S.A., is Bryce Canyon, a huge abyss which opens up on a fir-covered plateau at an altitude of 8,200 feet.*

4-5 *The New York skyline stands out against the horizon. The panorama of United States metropolises is characterized by skyscrapers, which have become famous for their particular architectural forms.*

6 *A cowboy having a break at sunset beside a giant cactus is one of the most common images of the West: a man, his horse, and nature.*

7 *Like solitary, majestic giants, the high natural reliefs of Monument Valley loom over a desert rendered arid by the burning sun. The Navajo Indians, who once lived on this land, gave these imposing natural towers strange names which were sometimes infantile and rather irreverent.*

8-9 *The Preservation Hall Jazz Band is one of the symbols of New Orleans' musical tradition.*

10-11 *San Francisco at night is lavish with lights and promises thousands of after-midnight entertainment opportunities, as one might expect from such a lively city which is so symbolic of a certain part of the west coast and so free from social prejudice.*

12-13 *Daytona Beach, in Florida, is 24 statute miles long and is frequented by young people who arrive in unusual vehicles. The sandy base is so compact that cars and motorcycles can be parked almost down to the water line.*

14-15 *Oak Alley is the most famous plantation in Louisiana. Built in 1750 by a family of French origin, it is approached along a splendid drive lined by centuries-old oak trees whose trunk circumference is, in some cases, equal to 33 feet.*

This edition published in 1996 by SMITHMARK Publishers, a division of U.S. Media Holdings Inc., 16 East 32nd Street, New York, NY 10016.

SMITHMARK books are available for bulk purchase for sales promotion and premium use. For details write or call the manager of special sales, SMITHMARK Publishers, 16 East 32nd Street, New York, NY 10016; (212) 532-6600.

First published by Edizioni White Star. Title of the original edition: America, il Paese del grande sogno. © World copyright 1993 by Edizioni White Star. Via Candido Sassone 24, 13100 Vercelli, Italy.

ISBN 0-8317-4830-3

Printed in Singapore by Tien Wah Press.

Introduction

There is a pseudo-psychological game which we all play sooner or later – that of free association of ideas. One person says a word, "family," for example, and another replies with the first thing that comes into his head, giving voice to the image the idea of family creates in his mind. One can say, "mother," or "house," or "warmth," or "argument"; it will always be a part of ourselves that comes to the surface. If 100 individuals of different ages, social class, sex, cultural background, family role, and job were to play the the game of free association starting with the words "United States of America," we would probably hear 100 different replies, some of which would be in total opposition to others. This happens because there is no single archetype to which we can make reference.

A land of obvious contrasts, a living paradox, or hell, however one wants to define it, the United States sums up, coagulates, and reveals the multiple and contradictory expressions of the planet earth. Unfortunately, the process of assimilation of so many different realities is still a long way from being complete. The United States continuously sends out harsh images of tentacular metropolises like New York and Los Angeles, in which the human condition is reduced and ground into a sort of self destruction, and soft images of small towns like those in Vermont, in which it is pleasant to come into contact with other human beings, following a style of life that is in harmony with the elementary and cyclical rhythms of nature and safeguarded by the rules which the community has established for itself.

Modern-day America presents a many-faceted reality. It is that freezing, rag-covered bundle sleeping in the New York subway; it's the beautiful surfer riding the waves at Big Sur; it's the entire family from a small town in Nevada spending the weekend at Las Vegas playing Keno, or enjoying the Magic Kingdom of Disneyworld. The United States is all-encompassing, take it or leave it.

Where nature has not thought about creating

differences, with its various combinations of vegetation and climate, fauna and territorial morphology, man has intervened. He lives crushed together in immense urban agglomerates like New York City, with a population of seven million, or reappropriates his individual living space in a state like Utah which has a population density of 15 people per square mile. The population density in North America is, in fact, on average much lower than that in Europe, and America really is the land of open spaces and long roads which cut across the country like arteries, starting from the most vital organs of the system – the cities.

The tourist who decides to visit the U.S.A. and who has no time limit is advised to use the bus or a car and to avoid air travel, which, although it is reasonably cheap and shortens the distances, does not allow the visitor to explore the landscape. In a country which, from East to West, has four different time zones,

(Eastern, Central, Mountain, and Pacific, each with a difference of an hour from the next), and which extends from the glaciers of Alaska to the Arizona desert and to the warm beaches of Florida (by no mere chance known as the Sunshine State) the visitor who travels by bus or by car has the opportunity of seeing many different varieties of landscape.

The North American landscape has been greatly modified since the arrival of the European colonists a little over two centuries ago. Then, over half of the total surface was covered in forests and now only 32 per cent of the country consists of "green" areas. However, it is still true that the U.S. boasts uncontaminated and extensive wooded areas. In New England there is a mixed vegetation of evergreen conifers and deciduous trees as well as many broadleaf trees, including the magnificent sugar maples of Vermont and New Hampshire, which illuminate the autumn with shades of gold and carmine. Farther to the south, the swampy areas are characterized principally by the mangroves of Florida. Proceeding west, the prairies mingle with oak woods, especially near lakes and other waterways. Moving ever farther West, the prairies provide seemingly endless panoramas and re-create those images of America for which a certain type of film has prepared us. In the southwest, the typical vegetation of Joshua trees and saguoro cactus reminds us that life also "flowers" in the desert. To the north, across the Californian coastal ridge, Douglas firs and enormous Sequoia tell other stories and fill us with new emotions.

Naturally, in the same way as the vegetation presents itself to the visitor in all its variety, the morphology of the terrain also presents diversities. Thus, a visitor to the tropical paradise of the Everglades in Florida might find it hard to believe that he is still in the same country which contains the Colorado basin with its more than 190,000 square miles of plateau and such natural architectural marvels as the Grand Canyon, Bryce's Canyon, and Death Valley. The same disorientation might be encountered by a visitor who decided to follow the course of the Mississippi River from its source to the mouth. This river is known as the"Brown Giant," because it is coloured by enormous quantities of detritus and eroded earth. It leaves Lake Minnesota and crosses the meadows of Wisconsin and the prairies of Iowa and Illinois before flowing through the savanna and quicksands of the delta, disappearing into the many "bayous" (marshy canals which form offshoots from the riverbed) of Louisiana and finally ending up in the warm waters of the Gulf of Mexico.

Naturally, in a country consisting of 50 states with a surface area of 3,600,000 square miles, there is a great variety of different landscapes, but what is even more disconcerting is the infinite and unequaled contradictoriness of the United States "system." The image which the U.S. has always evoked is that of a well-to-do and efficient white society with some ethnic minorities – black, Hispanic, and Oriental communities whose members suffer in their roles as manual laborers or chronic unemployed. This image ought to be replaced with a perception of North American reality which is much more faceted and complex. Indeed, the futuristic example of a truly multiracial society is already a reality in the United States, especially in the large cities.

Even within the white, Anglo-Saxon group which speaks American (one cannot define it as English), the living conditions are extremely diversified. The division between white-collar and blue-collar workers is really very clear, even among the white population. Levels of unemployment reach peaks of 10 per cent without great distinctions between race and sex. In the cities

18-19 *The Niagara Falls are not the highest in the world, nor have they the greatest flow of water. However, they are one of the ten most photographed places in the world and are second only to New York City as a tourist attraction in the United States.*

unfortunately, the contrast between the wretched living conditions of the weak who are left to their own devices and the comfortable conditions of those who participate in the raging consumerism is also mirrored in the subdivision of quarters. The charred houses of the South Bronx partially dim the shining lights of the display windows of stores such as Gucci, Cartier, and Tiffany along Fifth Avenue, and a visit to Park Avenue does not blot out the image of the "have-not" begging on the subway.

Criminality is widespread, with a yearly increase of 10 per cent in the number of common offenses committed in New York alone. The New York City administration spent $700 million on drug prevention measures in 1986. Today, that figure has risen to $900 million, because the widespread diffusion of crack has led to an enormous increase in the number of drug addicts.

In big cities, such as New York, Los Angeles, or Miami one can live or die under the watchful eyes of the world, with a sort of indifference that is so disconcerting as to seem almost natural. Armies of "integrated" people in business suits, who take the train every day to go to work in Manhattan, cannot cancel the breathtaking official estimate which informs us that there are at least 550,000 habitual users of hard drugs, such as heroin and crack, in New York City. This statistic does not even consider those who make use of the so-called "light drugs".

The inhuman dimension of the metropolises does not, however, prevent the residents of the small cities or the numerous farms dotted throughout the land from enjoying their status as Americans with pride and patriotic optimism. America is no longer the same country that was once viewed as a Promised Land by the millions of immigrants who were processed at Ellis Island in New York. It is no longer a land which guarantees a better future to those who want to prosper and who have that energy so much admired by the pioneers. This is precisely because the internal social and political situation is not the same as that of the dizzy ascent which the United States experienced between the end of the last century and the start of the great depression in 1929. However, the Americans, or at least the typical American, believes in his country, offers his sons to the homeland, still flees from the odor of communism and, above all, boasts of the fact that widely differing ethnic groups are represented, in different percentages, within American society.

The Chicanos, called "wetbacks" because they usually cross the border by swimming across the Rio Grande del Norte, are part of America. Emerging and well-off blacks, who are sometimes called "peacocks" because of their garish elegance, are also America. So are the blue-collar workers who belong to a large lower

middle class group of skilled workers, craftsmen, and small traders. Blacks who have been unemployed for generations or who live waiting for their habitual pusher to bring them a daily dose which might turn out to be their last one, are also America. America is also those thousands of orientals, mainly Chinese, who originally arrived around 1850 when the west coast was ready to welcome an influx of low-wage manual laborers to help in the building of the railroad. Today, on the whole, they live in the Chinatowns of cities such as San Francisco and New York, but also in smaller towns where they work hard to become fully-fledged citizens of the country which hosts them.

The Indians are also an aspect of America. The story of the American Indian is a separate chapter in the multi-racial history of the country and as such it must be treated. Bear in mind that, unlike the blacks, who, like the Orientals were originally imported for reasons of pure profit, or the Hispanics, who were simply looking for a way out of their precarious and unhappy living conditions, the Indians were the first inhabitants of the country. They came from Siberia during the last glaciation, when the Bering Strait still linked the Asian and American continents. These nomads from the east were the true discoverers of America. They lived in full and peaceful contact with the land, hunting or farming in those places where the land was more fertile, and they reached a rather high level of civilization, developing different languages from common roots, preferring the activity of fishing along the Pacific coast, and the cultivation of crops such as beans, pumpkins, tomatoes, sweet potatoes, and cocoa in the interior. The redskins' welcome of the European explorers and then the new indigenous peoples, the "Americans," was repaid with a policy that almost led to their extinction. From 1887 to 1934, the law for the allocation of land reduced from 55 million to 20 million the number of hectares of land possessed by the Indians. And, until 1968, the declarations of the Bill of Rights were denied to the Indians.

The same thing happened to them as happened to their companions on the prairies, the bison. In 1902, the U.S. Congress allocated $50,000 to save the last herd of 21 bison in Yellowstone Park from extinction. This tragic event was predictable if one considers that, back in 1883, the hunting of the bison by the white man had forced William "Buffalo Bill" Cody to ask the Philadelphia Zoo to lend him a couple of bison so that he could take his Wild West show to Europe. The disappearance of the bison was due to the breaking of a delicate equilibrium, which then had serious consequences for the way of life of the Indians, who thus lost their totem animal, the symbol of divine favor granted to them after the performance of propitiatory rites. The bison was dying, and Congress tried to find a

20 top *Hemingway's House, in Spanish-colonial style, has now been turned into a museum and has become one of the principal attractions of Key West in Florida. This island has hosted many famous people in the past, like President Truman and the writers Tennessee Williams and Don Passos. The most popular name, however, remains that of Hemingway, who had a particularly fruitful creative period when he was here.*

20 bottom *Only the blue sea and sky surround Key West. In the second half of the 19th century, this island rivaled Havana in the export of tobacco. However, with the 1929 recession, Key West began to exploit its climate and tropical vegetation as well as the practice of deep-sea fishing.*

21 top *The Florida Keys extend into the Gulf of Mexico for more than 125 miles and consist of 42 small islands.*

21 bottom *Seven Miles Bridge links Big Pine, covered with pine trees, cactus, and a profusion of palms, to the tourist resort of Marathon. All 42 of the Florida Keys are connected by a network of highways known as Overseas Highway, with many bridges suspended over the water.*

remedy for this situation.

The white man had not shown as much solicitude towards the first inhabitants of the large country. In 1902, when the untimely but effective intervention of the government enabled the repopulation of the bison, only 12 years had passed since the massacre at Wounded Knee. The slaughter of 200 defenseless Indians was the price which was paid for the end of the Seventh Cavalry at Little Big Horn in 1876. The Indians, however, never managed to get their revenge. On that evening of December 19, 1890, the Sioux lost much more than Big Foot and his 200 companions. Annihilated, humiliated, and reduced to silence, they lost their identity and their pride as a people. From that moment onward, the American Indians have lived a largely unfavorable existence which is threatened by endemic problems such as alcoholism, unemployment, discrimination, and even suicide. Today the people of the United States feel a strong sense of responsibility for what they have done. The stereotype image of angry, scalp-hunting Indians who show no pity for defenseless women and children is now obsolete and there is now real interest in the Indian cause. Proof of this fact is that, in recent years, American cinema has changed the contents of what it transmits to the collective imagery of the country and now shows, the history of this genocide with harsh verisimilitude.

Like the Indian question, other subjects which were at one time considered off-limits by producers, such as mixed marriages, the break-up of the family, and social conflicts, have been brought to the attention of the general public thanks to efforts of small production companies who are willing to take risks and produce controversial films. Hollywood, as it has been passed down to us by its own myth, is really only a memory. The dream factory no longer lives on the hill in Los Angeles. Nostalgic fans can visit Hollywood Memories to photograph the set costumes of Bogart in *Casablanca* or of Judy Garland in *The Wizard of Oz*, or they can visit Paramount Gate (the entrance seen in the film *Sunset Boulevard*). One can also roam around the 34 studios at Universal, turning pale in front of the 22-foot-long shark from the film *Jaws* and feeling a shiver run down one's spine at the sight of the house from *Psycho*, but Hollywood is certainly no longer what it once was. A certain type of cinema, created by omnipotent producers such as Selznick, Mayer, and Goldwyn, and based on a star system which bridled the existence of the actors by making them sign one-sided contracts and even forcing them to create unacceptable fictions in their private lives, and a type of cinema which outrageously adulterated reality and was governed by moralistic prescriptions (such as, for example, the notorious "Hays Code" in the 1950s) no longer exists.

Everything changes unexpectedly in the United

States more than in Europe or the rest of the world. The social problems become enormous and society radically alters its rules or breaks them without managing to find suitable replacements for them. Cities like Los Angeles, San Francisco, Atlanta, Miami, and New York live on ephemeral fashions and "upside down" myths like the quest for money, the mania for efficiency, and the love of the body which is viewed as a perfectable machine. Competition in the professional world and in commerce knows no scruples, there a general indifference to traditional values, and a precariousness in interpersonal relations.

Unfortunately, the expression "there are two sides to every coin" perfectly mirrors the situation. The admiration for human cultural achievements which is engendered by a visit to the Metropolitan or the Guggenheim Museums , the almost childlike joy aroused by a visit to Chinatown during the Chinese New Year are in sharp contrast to the emotions created by a visit to those streets of the metropolis dedicated to the "sale of bodies". For a few dollars one can "buy" any type of sexual encounter in Soho, New York, or on Bourbon Street in New Orleans.

New Orleans normally conjures up idyllic images of a pleasurable city which is one of the symbols of the South, in which 19th-century colonial style residences adorned with flowered porches and charming balconies, form a backdrop to the musical bands which march in measured steps across Jackson Square. It evokes the atmosphere of the deep South with the unbridled gaiety which pervades the city during "Mardi Gras," and the tasty local cuisine (a splendid mixture of French, South-American and Spanish cookery known as Creole cuisine. All this, however, barely conceals the most secret reality of this city of pleasure where the gay community is second in size only to that of San Francisco.

New Orleans still has the sleepy charm of a typical southern city which the march of progress has decisively eliminated in other cities. The style of the old Creole city can still be found almost intact in the old French Quarter or "Vieux Carr." A particularly splendid example of Creole architecture is the Cabildo, once headquarters of the Spanish Dominion. It has typically Spanish-style arcades to which a typical French mansard roof has been added. Also in French and "Cajun" style, with colored plaster-work, porticoes, and balconies framed with lacy wrought-iron grillwork, are the town homes in the prestigious Pontalba Buildings, which date from 1849. Formerly these were the residences of the French aristocracy and of great writers like William Faulkner and Sherwood Anderson, who lived in New Orleans.

For those who wish to take a real step back in time, Jackson Square brings to mind many historic events such as the French colonial settlement, public

22 top *The "Pueblo" of Taos, New Mexico is characterized by typical dwellings made of unfired bricks. Near these houses, the Indians display the manufactured goods which they sell to supplement the income they make from cultivating the fields.*

22 bottom *Many of the Cherokee Indians who live in North Carolina work in factories which produce moccasins. Others, like the woman in the picture, produce pretty objects with their skilled hands.*

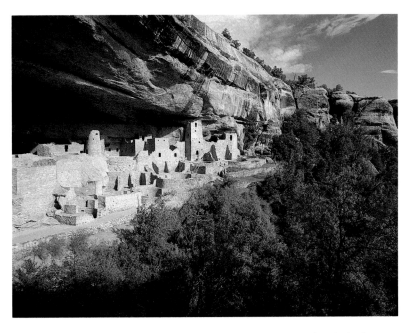

23 *Visitors to the archaeological zone of Mesa Verde, in Colorado, can see examples of the primitive dwellings which the Indians dug in the rock mor than a thousand years ago. As well as the famous ruins of Cliff Palace, one can also visit an immense "kiva," an underground temple of a troglodytic pueblo religious community.*

executions, and the Louisiana Purchase, in which the United States bought the whole of Louisiana from Napoleon in 1803 for $15 million. Today, many jazz concerts are held in Jackson Square, and every year there is a parade of allegorical floats during Mardi Gras celebrations. In New Orleans the carnival season explodes shortly after Christmas and reaches its peak on Shrove Tuesday. Locals and tourists all participate actively in the general bustle and in the dances, filling the French Quarter as well as St. Charles Avenue and Canal Street.. In the same period, many private receptions are attended by groups of formally dressed couples in evening suits and long gowns in the truly magnificent dwellings between First and Third streets.

Another splendid town about 124 miles away is Natchez in the state of Mississippi. Here, even more than in New Orleans, time seems to have stood still. Some 20 mansions in the style of *Gone with the Wind* offer southern hospitality to visitors. These include the splendid Stanton Hall, built around 1850 by a cotton magnate, as well others with names like Melrose, Rosalie, Linden, and Monmouth. Many of these residences contain real treasures of antique furniture, and during the "Natchez Pilgrimage" in March and in October they welcome paying guests to picturesque costume balls. These events coincide with the flowering of the magnificent azaleas and the vivid explosion of autumnal colors: and so nature also participates in this gala of local architecture.

The origin of Natchez as a tourist city dates back to the 1930s, when some local ladies tried to refill the family coffers which had diminished during the depression by welcoming paying visitors to their dwellings. Even today, the tours of the past continue successfully. Candlelight parties and ladies in crinoline add to the splendor of Stanton Hall, which still contains the original furniture imported from Europe in 1850, as well as to the Art Museum in Coctow House and the Dress Museum in Magnolia Hall. The Natchez Trace begins at Natchez. This is an incredible 446 mile-long panoramic road which was an Indian trail 8,000 years ago and in the last century was used by travelers going North towards the Mississippi basin. The trail continues to Nashville, Tennessee, and represents a charming itinerary for those who wish to leave the deep South behind and travel directly to the musical heart of America.

As is known, in the United States the musical adventure runs along the notes of blues, country, jazz, soul, and funky rock. All that is best in modern music was invented here. Music is everywhere: it can be heard in city parks when improvised groups assemble spontaneously; it accompanies shopping in large department stores; it provides the soundtrack to hundreds of sporting, ceremonial, theatrical, celebrative, and purely fun events which take place in the country. A musical journey could begin in Chicago, home of electric urban blues which has reinvigorated the original and unrefined blues of the countryside, and move on to acid rock which one imagines as the natural accompaniement to the "happenings" of the 1970s in San Francisco. From there it might pass through Memphis, where Elvis Presley's home Graceland reminds us that rock and roll was born in this Tennessee town on the borders of Mississippi and Arkansas.In New Orleans the ragtime music played by small bands mingles with the jazz loved by so many of the city's inhabitants. Black jazz musicians are known locally as "professors."

New York City is a mecca for rising musical talents. The "Village Voice" is the official organ of the musical movement in the Big Apple. Every week, its pages act as a tom-tom calling the omnivorous musical people of New York to restructured cellars, "trendy" discotheques, "off" and "off off" Broadway theatres as well as private clubs such as the one in which Woody Allen has been known to play his clarinet. At "Folk City," with its memories of Dylan, and at "Bottom Line," in which punk and new wave music are often played, one encouters a heterogeneous group of people made up of night owls who live from midnight onward, those passionately fond of a particular kind of music, tourists looking for metropolitan excitement, the most severe and influential critics, artists, and a certain circle of intellectuals. Jazz is king in Harlem, although it is the Newport Jazz Festival, held in spring or at the beginning of the summer, that attracts the most significant musicians of the moment. Central Park, an outdoor arena with a maximum capacity of 4,000 spectators, is the setting for numerous concerts, and Madison Square Garden certainly does not need advertising hype.

Nashville, however, wins the prize as musical city par excellence. This is because it literally lives from music, with about 100 recording studios, 40 musical publishing houses, and a large number of promotion agencies for would-be or well established singers. As promised by the welcome signs, Nashville is really "Music City, U.S.A." and, in fact, half of all the records produced in America are recorded here. There are all the spin-off activities such as bookshops and stores selling souvenirs and gadgets to increase the huge turnover linked to show business. One event has a particular resonance – the Grand Ole Opry, which takes its name from a well-known radio program. The show takes place on the stage of the Opry House and attracts guitarists who are a bit behind the times and blonde country singers in the style of Dolly Parton, applauded every weekend, in the two shows held on Fridays and Saturdays, by crowds of fans who come from all corners

24 *The nocturnal panoramas of the main streets of American tourist resorts present an enormous variety of neon signs, including motels offering very cheap rates, bars and restaurants offering their specialities, or shops advertising their products.*

of the United States. It is of little importance that Robert Altman unmasked the respectable myth which was at the base of the good, healthy country music loved by all good Americans: Nashville is really a phenomenon which, to tell the truth, attracts an enormous quantity of people and thus deserves the respect due to a structure which is so successful at selling itself.

On the other hand, "wonder cities" are legitimized by the success and the great pleasure which they provide, and all one has to do is to go to Las Vegas, the realm of gambling, or Disneyworld, the kingdom of fantasy and good feelings, to realize the truth of this statement. Las Vegas has 200,000 inhabitants and is a real city even without counting the 12 million tourists who visit it every year. Disneyland and Disneyworld are two small "cities" with little more than several tens of thousands of inhabitants each. All three of them are mythical cities and are emblematic of that which collective imagery understands by the American "dream." They are representative of that typical United States tendency to concentrate passions such as gambling, the quest for fortune and easy money, or innocent family entertainment into islands and watertight compartments. It is for this reason that the best known travel agencies which offer "coast to coast" trips always propose a visit to Disneyworld, a short trip to Las Vegas, and a trip to Disneyland.

Of these two very well known amusement parks, Disneyland was the first to be founded, in 1955, on the west coast near Los Angeles. Disneyworld was its logical continuation at Orlando in Florida on the east coast 15 years later. From 1955 to date, more than 300 million visitors have paid the entrance toll in "Disney dollars" with the effigy of Donald Duck's uncle, to enter the fable of Disneyland. They have walked along Main Street, entering the atmosphere of a small city in the Midwest at the start of this century, and walked on without pause between the pastel-colored houses of New Orleans Square, boarded the 19th-century train on the Thunder Mountain Railroad, which enters the mines of the gold diggers, and savored the panorama of the Mark Twain Steamboat, which simulates a large paddle steamer cruising down the placid waters of the Mississippi. In Adventureland, the tourist is then immersed in a luxuriant vegetation without precise morphological or geographic features which promises encounters (albeit fleeting) with hungry cannibals and tigers on the lookout for a succulent meal. In the House of Spirits, a good shudder of fear is guaranteed by high-definition special effects in the same way that great excitement will be supplied by the monumental big dipper known as the Magic Mountain. All the charm of those adventure stories read during childhood will be re-evoked in the section dedicated to the Caribbean

25 *American buildings are sometimes characterized by a rather bizarre taste: such is the case with this service station in Louisiana and this dinosaur-shaped auto center, captured by the photographer's lens at the side of a road in Florida.*

pirates. The visit to Disneyland will conclude with the boarding of the space shuttle Endor Express at Tomorrowland. The waiting room of the airport promises interstellar voyages and close encounters of every type, and if one bears in mind that the director of the production was Disney Corporation under the supervision of George Lukas, creator of *Star Wars*, a good journey is guaranteed. Everything is carefully simulated, the annoying pressure on the seat during blast-off, the sudden turns to avoid unexpected obstacles, the speed "of light," the firey showering of a thousand meteorites, the sudden nose-ups and swerves of the shuttle, the plunge into a shaft of crystal, and the ambush by the fleet of the Empire of Evil. When the impact with the enemy seems inevitable, there is a surprise explosion, and the opening of the landing doors reduces everything to realistic proportions. It was only a game, albeit the most spectacular one of Disneyland. Naturally, when Disneyworld was planned 15 years later, every attempt was made to surpass Disneyland and today, as well as the six "theme parks" which make up the Magic Kingdom, there is a model town with five lakes, numerous tennis courts , golf courses, a nature reserve of 4,000 hectares, several hotels, and two railway lines. That's not all. The resort hotel complex outside the Magic Kingdom rises up 15 floors to form a gigantic letter "A" crossed by a monorail which was planned and built by Disney; the 1,046 rooms of the Contemporary Hotel are soundproofed and equipped with automatic sprinklers in case of fire, and they even have artificial moonlight.

But the cherry on the cake is the large underground section of the Magic Kingdom which contains water conduits and electricity cables and above all serves for the transit of vehicles and the bringing in of supplies and articles of everyday need, without disturbing the happy atmosphere of play and fable which reigns supreme on the surface. More than 50 tons of garbage are channeled into the Automated Vacuum Collection System and transported rapidly to an incinerator which is a short distance away from the entertainment park. The drainage water, used to sustain the numerous and luxuriant Florida plants in the nursery, is filtered and purified with an advanced recycling system based on high level technological innovations. It was built to create the "Community of Tomorrow," so dear to the Disney idea of Utopia, flanking the fanciful illusions of the Magic Kingdom with a reality which is also a hope and a faith in the increasing capacity of man to improve the world he inhabits and to optimize the system thanks to the aid of its best talents, be they the patient creators of the most famous animated drawings on five continents or the most creative and "advanced" scientists of their time.

Disney's is an optimistic American dream, but

26 top *The night traffic on San Francisco's Golden Gate Bridge traces brilliant "cables" of light.*

26 bottom *The intersecting of many thoroughfares reminds one that it is impossible to live without a car in Los Angeles. Only with an automobile can one cover the enormous distances which separate the different parts of this megalopolis.*

27 top *Lombard Street, in San Francisco, forms ten hairpin curves which are edged by flower beds full of hydrangeas.*

27 bottom *Speed limits on American roads are rather low, and the maximum limit is 55 mph. This picture shows the highway which goes to Atlanta.*

28-29 *A seaplane cuts through the waves in Miami, Florida.*

30-31 *In spite of the recent competition from Atlantic City, Las Vegas remains the world's most popular gambling spot.*

paradoxically, America relates and expresses itself also in the adult amusement park of Las Vegas, along the mile-long street known as "the Strip," the most brightly illuminated street in the world, whose dazzling multicolored signs can be seen at distances of up to 60 miles. The origin of Las Vegas' wealth is the result of a Nevada state law which, beginning in the 1930s, enabled couples to obtain a divorce within a few weeks and made it equally easy to speed up the procedures for getting married. Thanks to these facilitations, an army of people wanting a divorce flew into Las Vegas, which prepared itself to welcome them with thousands of slot machines, innumerable blackjack tables and, in short, all the instruments which permitted the wait for the divorce to be passed pleasurably. Since then, the capital of entertainment has added other strings to its bow, diversifying the offers provided by its excellent restaurants, casinos and hotels which host world famous stars. The tourist can choose between the Bacchanal Room, which reproduces a Roman villa from the times of Augustus, in Caesar's Palace Hotel, the Gigi Cafe in the MGM Hotel, which simulates the interiors of the costume film "Marie Antoinetta," or even the Carson City Restaurant in the Circus Hotel, where the diners sit around an arena in which trapeze artists, clowns, and acrobats perform. The majority of money changes hands around traditional tables of dice, blackjack or roulette or is played in slot machines, video poker machines, and video formula one races as well as competitions against robots which have been electronically programmed to make things challenging. Gambling, which is favored psychologically by the absence of clocks and windows so as not to give the players any rest, remains the real protagonist and brings to the city and to Nevada more than two billion dollars a year. The fact that Las Vegas is preparing to become an important convention center in the 1990s is the result of that typical American business sense, but, for most people, it remains the city of gambling and intends to remain so for a long time to come.

Death Valley is about 130 miles from Las Vegas, on the borders of Nevada and California. In its Dantesque landscape, the presence of man is merely an accessory. Here, nature is the protagonist, not only because of the unusual beauty of the landscape, which includes the gold and purple of the Golden Canyon, the ochre of Mustard Canyon, the red, green, and brown of the Black Mountains and the multi-colored pebbles of the Mosaic Canyon, but above all because of the solemn and almost lunar atmosphere which the natural elements created about three million years ago, between the end of the Pliocene period and the beginning of the Quaternary era. Here, erosion by atmospheric agents and huge volcanic eruptions have created an infinite series of reliefs. Some of these are rocky and jagged like Artist 's

Palette while others are more rounded like the dunes which color the horizon with yellow, orange, mother of pearl, and ochre. There are darker brushstrokes where the plants with very deep roots form flashes of color in an arid universe which still palpitates, lives, and forcefully imposes its beauty. Death Valley extends over an area of almost 7,000 square miles in the Mojave Desert. The Indians originally called it Tomesha (Land of Fire) and it was given its current name after the tragic event which happened to a group of gold diggers who succumbed to the infernal heat of the desert on their way to California in 1849. Yet, despite its funereal name, the hidden charm of this valley are to be found on starry nights when the heat lets up and the valley's numerous inhabitants come into the open; among these are goat antelope and wild mules which are the descendants of those famous convoys of 20 mules which brought sodium borate out of the valley at the time of the pioneers. There are also many species of birds including geese, heron, and ducks which visit the small marshes to be found in this vast territory. Human presence in the happy desert, as it has been defined, is very low and there are only 200 residents, the majority of whom are employed in the national park or in one of the two hotels in the region. Human intervention has been limited by the "impossible" climate, with summer temperatures of more than 50° C, but perhaps an intelligent limit has been placed on the use of the territory, and, with due respect to the natural treasures, country roads and structures have been built only where necessary.

America has always felt that its greatest richness was its territory, protagonist of so many western films, that land where palefaced horsemen hid themselves behind the pinnacles of Monument Valley, or rode on mules from one side of the Grand Canyon to the other, traveled up and down the wide prairies of the West, and hunted for bounty to the southwest in the Sonora Desert. Therefore, the United States began to preserve its natural resources from the more evil inhabitants when the concept of ecology had not yet been formulated. Indeed, in 1872, Yellowstone Park became the first national park in the country's history. A park with 200 geysers and 3,000 hot springs, waterfalls, and streams, terraces of travertine stone, swamps and stalactites, thousands of animals including bison, deer, elk, marmots, eagles, and falcons, on display against a backdrop of extremely varied natural beauty almost as if Yellowstone were trying to offer in its 9,000 square miles a sample of all natural marvels. Every year the park is visited by millions of people, and the risk of commercialization is thus very high, but for the moment the characteristics of Yellowstone have been maintained by the people who work in this sector.

Another precaution, albeit a little late, forbids the

collecting of fossils in the Petrified Forest Park, in Arizona. This area of 143,000 sqaure miles contains the largest collection of petrified wood in the world, and here the only color which does not appear is green. The desert landscape may seem inhospitable, consisting as it does of dead trees which have been turned into stone, but it has its own particular beauty and especially in the giant logs the magnificent colors highlight the incredible process of petrification, which began 70 million years ago and which caused the trunks to color themselves as splinters of onyx, agate, and jasper. Once again, it is Arizona which contains perhaps the most famous national park in the U.S.A., the Grand Canyon National Park. Of the 19 canyons which follow the course of the Colorado river from its source in the Rocky Mountains to its mouth in the Gulf of California, these 1,930 square miles contain the most spectacular geological structures, whose projection and shape are due to the erosion of the sedimentary strata which the river created five or six million years ago. The dominant colors are, as one might imagine, ochre and sienna, and the shapes bear witness to the forces of nature which modeled them in a few moments of unheard-of thrusting or by means of a slow progression which has lasted millions of years. Everything speaks of the greatness of nature, and those who do not like technical calculations and scientific explanations can place their trust in the almost mystic emotion which the sight of the Grand Canyon provokes, especially those who observe it from above, from an airplane or a helicopter.

On the border between Arizona and Utah we find that which cannot exactly be defined as an American park, but which quite rightly claims the title of an Indian Park – Monument Valley. In fact, it rises at the heart of the Navajo reserve, and it is the Indians who offer their services as guides for trips into this valley which contains the splendid formations of red sandstone, the peaks of which are more than 984 feet high and which suddenly rise up from the surrounding flat desert and have formed the background to so many Western films. These natural "towers" are equal in form to the buildings of Manhattan, and probably the two opposing images equally attract the interest of the tourist or of those who like to travel at home in the mind and create their own America.

On the other hand, America is in equal measure the frenzied world which throngs in the densely populated quarters of such metropolises as Chicago, Los Angeles, and New York, and that large, spacious country which has space to sell to those who want to travel across it and experience it. The United States is such a composite and complex reality that it would be impossible to try to classify it into well defined categories. There is a working America consisting of world-famous factories

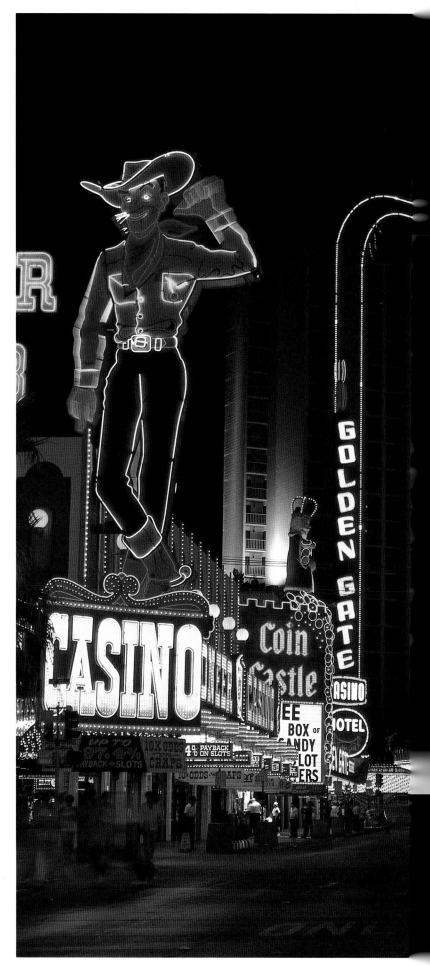

which boast highly advanced production systems, and there is a poor America which lives in squalid ghettos thanks to the handouts of the welfare system or at the mercy of exploiters in the slums. There is the America of West Point with its cadets in their white uniforms and the country of the huge peace marches; there is the America of television "serials" and more conventional "soap operas" and the America which listens to itself in the poetry readings of avant-garde artists. There is the America which lives with the break-up of the family and the America which is attempting to regain higher values through the proliferation of numerous religious sects; the robust and slightly coarse America of the rodeo and other great sporting occasions and the America which burns up its young generations. The United States is a cross-section of varied humanity of opposing mentalities which overlap in a contradictory fashion. America is everything and the opposite of everything, and if we were to play the game of free association starting with the words "United States of America," it would be very difficult to bet on how many would say "Manhattan" and how many would say "Grand Canyon."

A Country Without Frontiers

"America is also and above all open space. Large, boundless, wild stretches portray the innermost sense of the country—the Grand Canyon, a chisel of rocky sculptures of breathtaking beauty, and the Rocky Mountains, with their legends of trappers, bears, Indians. And on another lyrical side is Hawaii: a most varied nature, with the palms of Oahu, the beaches and lagoons of Waikiki, the luxuriant vegetation of Maui, the volcanoes, and the warning wrecks of armed ships in the deadly waterways of Pearl Harbor. Forests are to be found throughout the country, as well as plenty of wild beaches with flying birds and sprinklings of foam. Coral reefs run along the islands. And unprofaned glaciers are common in Alaska, turned into the last frontier for oil, the American Siberia."

Guido Gerosa

In 1938 John Ford discovered the incomparable scenario of Monument Valley, and in 1939 this was the setting for his masterpiece *Stagecoach*. It was not only the great success obtained from both critics and public which caused Ford to come back here to film *Fort Apache* in 1948, *She Wore a Yellow Ribbon* in 1949, *The Searchers* in 1956, and *Cheyenne Autumn* in 1964. In his films, the landscape was the absolute co-star alongside the cavalry soldiers and the fleeing Cheyennes. The fact that Ford repeatedly chose Monument Valley is extremely significant and highlights the spectacularity of this natural scenario in which gigantic cathedrals of stone rise up loftily from the tormented ground.

32 top and 33 *The heights of Monument Valley have particular and rather surreal names which were given them by the ancestors of the 30,000 Navajo Indians who still live here and do not want to leave.*

32 bottom *Landscapes sculpted in the rocks cover large areas of the American West. Twisting gorges form the beds of thousand-year-old rivers and bear witness to the remote geological process which produced the wild beauty of the Grand Canyon.*

The Valley of Stone Cathedrals

Landscapes which are literally sculpted into the rock cover the wide spaces of the American West. Twisting gorges, crossed by millenarian rivers' flow, bear witness to the remote geological processes which created the wild beauty of the Grand Canyon. The spirit which animated its creation seems to have remained imprisoned in the monolithic blocks of Monument Valley. Indeed, the most beautiful songs of the Navajo culture speak of the origin of the universe and of that force consisting of rain, wind, and lightning which molded the rocks and **desert**.

The Long Work
of the Centuries

36-37 *Canyonlands National Park extends for more than 250,000 acres in the state of Utah.*

37 top *The San Juan River as it enters Gooseneck State Reserve in Utah.*

37 bottom *An aerial view of Lake Powell and the Glen Canyon National Recreation Area in Utah.*

38-39 *The Grand Canyon, which President Theodore Roosevelt defined as "that superb panorama which every American should see," was formed by the erosion carried out by the Colorado River over the course of 30 million years. In addition, the United States contains many other spectacular landscapes created by the tireless action of nature.*

Another Planet

Death Valley extends over a territory of about 3,000 square miles, 580 of which are below sea level. Death Valley, which the Panamit Indians called "Land of Fire," takes its current name from the tragedy which befell a group of miners from Nevada who lost their lives in this desolate territory in 1849. The natural spectacle offered by this desert has no equal elsewhere in the

world. Sand dunes whose shapes are in continuous evolution alternate with arid valleys in which the sun-dried earth is cracked and split. The heights and the canyons take on a variety of hues, contrasting the blinding light of the sun with the strength of the centuries. The Devil's Golf Course represents the apotheosis of the wild and indomitable beauty of Death Valley: here, a bizarre genius seems to have created delirious sculptures of salt crystals which rise up spectrally from the ground.

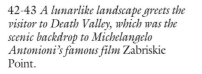

42-43 A lunarlike landscape greets the visitor to Death Valley, which was the scenic backdrop to Michelangelo Antonioni's famous film Zabriskie Point.

Trees in Prayer

Joshua Tree National Monument in California is a victory of naturalism over capitalism. It was created in 1936 as a protected area, despite pressures from mining companies who wanted to exploit the resources of the area. The name "Joshua Tree" was given by the first Mormon visitors in the 19th century, who saw, in the form of the yucca, a resemblance to Moses' successor, Joshua, at prayer.

45

Riding the Waves

Big Sur is that stretch of coast to the south of Monterey peninsula and Carmel-by-the-Sea. Monterey was the first capital of California, and among its former inhabitants was Robert Louis Stevenson, who stayed there in 1879 and perhaps drew inspiration for his stories of pirates and hidden treasures. The area is still rather wild, and there are many points at which one's gaze is lost between sky and sea. Carmel-by-the-Sea is a secluded place which has practically become a community of artists who prefer the quiet characteristic streets of this small town, in which neon signs are forbidden, to the bright signs and colorful shop windows of the majority of other towns. On the rocks of Carmel one can often see colonies of seals and sea lions which are accustomed to the presence of man. Here, nature still conserves its charms, and those who love the sea, without wishing the conveniences of the more crowded resorts, can have a pleasant stay. On the other hand, Big Sur is rather crowded and is perhaps the best known stretch of that Californian west coast that is known to all. The landscape, with its cliffs plummeting down to the sea, its highly irregular and indented coastline, and the beautiful ocean, merits the fame it has acquired. Big Sur is a mythical stopping-off point for those who love California and its ocean, but also for those who have fallen under the influence of a certain group of American intellectuals who founded a center here at Big Sur under the aegis of Henry Miller.

A Giant Park

Yosemite National Park extends over 2,980 statute miles of mountains, green valleys, and plain. It contains the largest monoliths in the world, real natural miracles such as Half Dome, El Capitan, North Dome, Sentinel, and Basket. It also includes Upper Fall, a waterfall which is much higher than Niagara, and Mariposa Grove, which contains sequoia trees with a diameter of more than 98 feet.

50-51 *The redwood trees (sequoia sempervirens) in Redwood National Park are the highest in the world, and here we also find the Tall Tree, universally acknowledged as being the tallest tree on earth.*

Uncontaminated Nature

Aspen, Colorado is the most prominent and best equipped downhill skiing resort of the entire West. The notoriously difficult slopes, the powdered snow, and the possibility of staying in the best hotels provide winter sports enthusiasts with everything their hearts could desire. However, despite the fact that it is a busy tourist area, the landscapes of Colorado still maintain a delightful and almost intact nature which also attracts visitors who are not particularly interested in practising sport. In these places one can return to nature, walking along almost deserted roads and fishing on the banks of lakes where there are few people.

Animals in Freedom

The fame of Yellowstone spread across the Atlantic a long time ago. This National Park, set up by President Ulysses S. Grant in 1872, is not only the oldest park in the United States but also the largest in the continental United States, with a surface area of 3,475 square miles. The majority of this territory is in Wyoming, but parts of it also extend into Idaho and Montana. The thing which really makes Yellowstone unique is its geothermal activity, with more than 200 geysers and almost 10,000 hot springs. The park contains the greatest concentration of geysers in the world, exceeding those in other regions such as Iceland, Siberia, and New Zealand. Moreover, it has a remarkable petrified forest in which the trees maintain the upright position which they had had millions of years ago when they were showered with volcanic ash and transformed. Very spectacular and of great interest is also the Grand Canyon of the Yellowstone River: from Artist's Point it is possible to admire the lower falls in all their splendor as they fall into the underlying gorge from a height of 108 feet. However, perhaps the major attraction of Yellowstone is that it provides the opportunity to see thousand of animals circulating freely, including deer, bears, elk, beavers, marmots, and coyote, as well as more than 200 species of birds such as the falcon, the rare whooper swan, and the bald eagle, symbol of the United States of America.

The Spirit of the South in a Great River

The Mississippi rises in Minnesota and curves its way through ten states before emptying into the Gulf of Mexico, where it forms a large delta of 17,760 square miles consisting mainly of marshy terrain, natural canals, and lakes. Despite the passage of time, this great river has maintained its extraordinary charm and its aristocratic elegance, which evoke in the soul all types of fantasies and magical sensations.

The Everglades, an Endless River of Grass

The region of the Everglades extends over an area of 1,300 square miles characterized by grassy stretches, swamps, and a rather hostile nature. In 1947, a national park of 2,300 square miles created. This is constantly patrolled by a well-trained corps of rangers who guarantee protection to a number of animals, including the manatee and the heron, which seem to be threatened with extinction.

Alaska, the Kingdom of Perennial Glaciers

Alaska has been quite rightly defined as the land of records. It is dotted with three million lakes; its "skeleton" consists of tens of thousands of islands and at least 270 glaciers which were formed in ancient times. Its clear skies are crossed by 9,000 aircraft; Alaska has an airplane for every 50 inhabitants and a pilot for every 42. The distances here are enormous, and overland travel is very difficult, especially in the colder season. The territory of Alaska extends over an area of 595,000 square miles, which is twice the size of Texas and equal to a fifth of the entire United States. From 1799 to 1867, this immense land, with its wealth of natural resources, was under Russian dominion before being sold to the Americans for about $7.2 million. In the second half of the last century, during the gold rush, Alaska was taken by storm by adventurers who dreamed of obtaining wealth quickly and easily. Among the pioneers, there was also a young writer destined for fame and glory – Jack London. In his stories he informed the world of the extraordinary uniqueness of these endless glaciers. Alaska is without doubt a strange country, dominated by enormous expanses of unpolluted tundra and taiga, in which caribou and wolves live in a self-regulating equilibrium which requires no human intervention. It was precisely for this reason that two million hectares were transformed into the Denali Nature Reserve, 248 statute miles south of the Arctic Circle, at the foot of the imposing mass of the 20141-feet-high Mt. McKinley.

Cities

"It is the fascination of the great American megalopolises which captures our imagination more than anything else. The influence of cinema and television have made Manhattan and Los Angeles seem more familiar to a young Italian than his home town. We can recognize the spire of the Chrysler skyscraper, or the house Frank Lloyd Wright built for Kaufmann, the Golden Gate and Brooklyn Bridges, and the Guggenheim Museum because they have been impressed on our mind's eye through the images of films, music and the photographs of *Life*."

Guido Gerosa

American cities, unlike European ones, are not linked to a well-defined and centuries-old history. However, their characters are nonetheless evident to the many ethnic groups who have had a part in their development, whether examined from the point of view of the very rich or the very poor.
Most of the cities pulsate with life, and echo to the sounds of the ever-present traffic, mingled with the voices of all the different peoples who have adopted the place as home.

64 top *The best view of the city of Seattle is to be had from the top of the rotating restaurant known as the Space Needle.*

64 bottom *The 4th of July celebrations in Philadelphia have a fundamental importance for every citizen. The celebrations are commensurate with the role this city played in the nation's history. In fact, the Declaration of Independence was signed at Philadelphia in 1776, and for a certain period, the city styled itself with the title of Capital.*

65 *The Empire State Building and the more recent World Trade Center, whose twin towers soar heavenward in the background, are among the best known symbols of New York.*

New York,
The Big Apple

"It's unique: its neuroses, its fever, its streets, which are dirty but luminous, smelly but perfumed, elegant but tumble-down, are the marvels of the world."

Guido Gerosa

To speak of this city in terms of figures is perhaps to impoverish it, but it should however be underlined that it has a population of about 7.5 million and that it is visited by 17 million tourists every year, making it the most popular tourist attraction in the western hemisphere. The complexity, variety, and contradictoriness of the Big Apple are excessive even for a New Yorker. In fact there is no archetype of New York, not even in that more or less deformed mirror which is the cinema.

The origins of New York date back to 1626, when the Dutchman Peter Minnewit bought the island of Manhattan from the Indians and founded a colony called New Amsterdam. The name New York was given by the English, who conquered the territory in 1664. Thanks to a particularly favorable geographic position, in the 17th century the city became the obligatory reference point for all those who arrived from Europe. Thus began the expansion of New York along with the birth of a great myth.

Washington, Style and Politics

Three buildings, built in symmetry and inserted into a context of parks and green areas, symbolize the original sense of the city of Washington when the capital had the role of safeguarding civil rights, individual rights, and independence. Overlooking the Potomac River is the Lincoln Memorial, with its 36 columns of white marble, representing the 36 states which formed part of the Union when it was built. Behind this is the obelisk, which reaches a height of 558 feet, and to its rear is Capitol Hill, seat of the Senate and the House of Representatives, symbol of the Federal Union and geometrical center of the city. These splendid buildings are set like gems into an exquisite architectural structure which, with its numerous neo-classical buildings, creates a perfect setting for the legend of Washington. Obviously, a must for any visitor to Washington is a tour of the White House, residence of the Head of State since 1800. George Washington commissioned the French architect Pierre Charles L'Enfant to lay out the city in 1791. A local law has decreed that no building over 13 stories may be built so that the Washington Monument will always be higher than any other building.

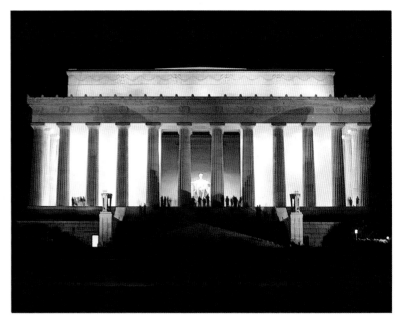

Los Angeles, City of Marvels

Incredibly, the first nucleus of Los Angeles was the Saint Gabriel Mission, founded by the Franciscan priests. The discovery of gold first, and then oil, combined to transform this small town into a large city which grows uncontrollably. In 1920 it was already the largest metropolis in the world, and in the 1950s Los Angeles reached the height of its economic expansion. More than any other city it represents the incarnation of success and of that American myth which has been the dream of whole generations. With its luxury villas, Beverly Hills represents the aspirations of millions of people, and Hollywood constitutes the materialization of the wildest dreams of fame and wealth.

74 *The circular towers of the Bonaventure Hotel, designed by architect John Portman, warmly reflect the light of the setting sun.*

75 left *Ultra-modern sculptures and daring constructions characterize the physiognomy of the financial district.*

75 top right *The tourist port for yachts at Marina del Rey is the largest on the Pacific coast and can hold more than 10,000 craft.*

75 bottom right *Los Angeles is a gigantic city, and its road network is more than 11,000 km long.*

76-77 *The city developed without a precise plan, and this led it to expand principally in a horizontal sense. Thus, its panorama is characterized by a vast expanse of low buildings above which rise the skyscrapers of the financial district.*

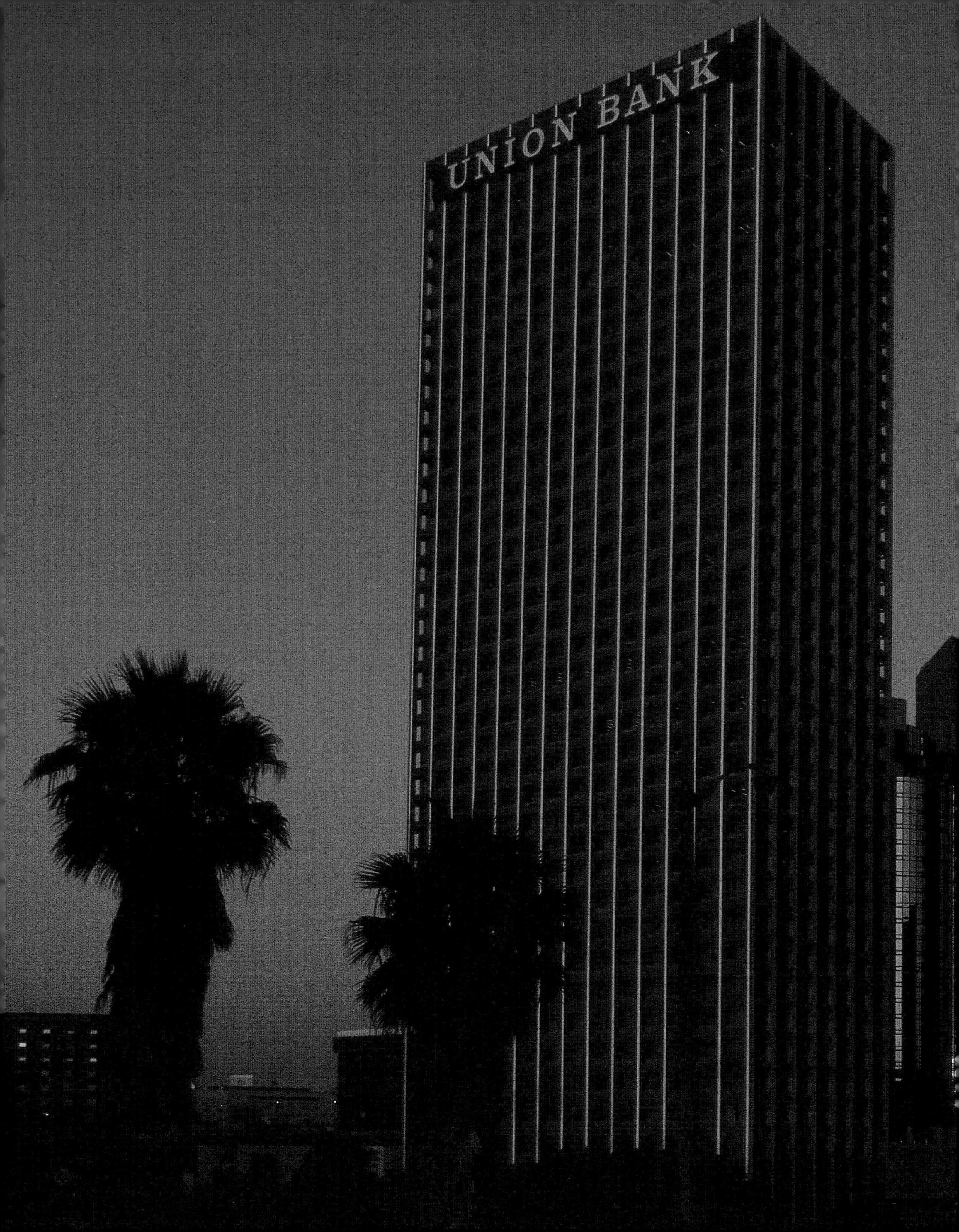
UNION BANK

San Francisco, Beautiful Place to Live

Resting, like Rome, on seven hills, with the Bay to the east and the Pacific Ocean to the west, San Francisco is blessed with a permanent breeze which does not allow the temperature to exceed 25° C. By choosing an inland suburb, one can also avoid the frequent coastal fog and enjoy the charming climate of San Francisco, venturing up and down the city's steep streets with their famous cable cars, one of

the best known features of the city. However, the true symbol of San Francisco is the Golden Gate Bridge, suspended 656 feet above the waves of the Pacific. Twelve rivers end their course under this bridge, which defies the forces of nature with its 20,000 tons of steel.

80-81 The Oakland Bay Bridge was opened to traffic in 1936. With a length of about 8 statute miles it links San Francisco and Oakland.

Chicago, The City of Impossible Challenges

It would be hard to find a city which could be defined as more American because of the frenzy and bustle which pervade Chicago, because of the efforts it makes to outdo itself in launching almost impossible challenges, and for the futurism glorified in its metropolitan architecture. Chicago is truly the city of economic supremacy, skyscrapers, and steel.

Boston, The Cultured City

Boston has been called the most European city in the United States, and when one strolls along Arlington Street where the rich Bostonians built their beautiful mansions and majestic churches, one realizes what is meant by European atmosphere. Here, where the Boston of Henry James maintains its characteristics, there is no exhibitionism nor a false note to disturb the harmonious equilibrium of the city.

New Orleans, City of Joy

The city whose emblem contains an old-fashioned grand piano clearly demonstrates its great love for music. However, this banner also reveals something else about New Orleans. The piano recalls the resistance offered by this confederate city in 1863 against the northern forces under General Sherman. The artillery of the Washington regiment placed this musical instrument in the

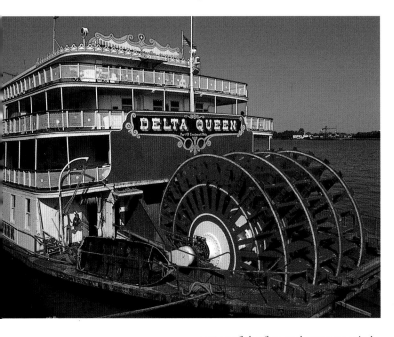

center of the fray and, accompanied by its notes, sang old patriotic songs before and after the attacks. The urban layout and the architectural style of the buildings are evident signs of the French and Spanish domination which alternated until 1803, when Napoleon sold the city to the United States of America. The most famous and certainly the most fascinating zone of the city is the Vieux Carr, the French Quarter, on the right bank of the Mississippi, which saw the birth of jazz at the start of the 20th century.

Dallas, The Rich "Big D"

Perhaps it is Dallas which holds the record for stereotypes in the United States. The image which springs to mind is that of the super-rich Texan with a cowboy hat who manages his many petroleum companies from the top of a modern glass skyscraper and who travels by Cadillac to reach his ranch just outside the city. This is partly true, since statistically, Dallas has the greatest number of luxury automobiles in the Western world, and the standard of living is quite high when compared with other cities, which have terrible areas of misery. It should, however, be remembered that oil alone is not sufficient to guarantee wealth and that behind a splendid landscape there is a productive reality based on hard work.

Miami, Millions and Art Deco

The most heterogeneous society in the United States is to be found in Miami. In particular, Cubans and Mexicans form a high percentage of the population, and it has indeed been estimated that half of the entire population speaks Spanish. Geographically, the city is divided by Biscayne Bay into two zones connected by the numerous highways and bridges which cross this stretch of internal sea.

From above, the surface of the water seems to be dotted with artificial islands on which there are luxury villas with private jetties and berths. Along with Miami Beach, Miami benefits from the wealth brought in by the tourist industry which has developed here thanks to the tropical climate and the luxuriant vegetation. Over the years, the city has created infrastructures which have no equal elsewhere in the world, with more than 500 hotels, 400 motels, and more than 4,000 restaurants. Many of these complexes were built by rich Cubans who fled their homeland between 1959 and 1960 with the fall of the Batista regime. In Little Havana, they have partially recreated the charming atmosphere of their country, developing one of the most picturesque corners of the city, pleasantly in contrast with the bright lights and modern architecture of the luxury hotels.

Honolulu, Paradise Regained

On the beaches of Waikiki, when King Kamehameha I conquered the territory of Oahu in 1795, the vegetation extended down to the shoreline, and in the surrounding area there were many fields interspersed with inhospitable swamps. Now, years later, the panorama has radically changed, and this beach has become one of the most representative symbols of international tourism.

Some 120,000 people live in an area of no more than 1.1 square miles, in which there are about 450 restaurants and 1,000 shops. The mythical Eden which nestled at the foot of Diamond Head, the extinct volcano which has become the symbol of Hawaii, has been transformed into a modern, rich, and cosmopolitan tourist paradise in which ancient traditions and customs, modified to serve the imperative needs of market and economy, struggle to survive. An eight-lane highway connects the airport to the city, and it is constantly full of traffic. At Honolulu, everything is geared to promoting the tourist industry, which is without a doubt the most important economic activity on the island and the principal source of employment for its inhabitants.

A Style of Life

"Every city and town in America is a world. The people in the United States have a multi-faceted dimension. A boundless planet and a human constellation without end which has undergone a ceaseless process of transformation in the last twenty years and is a source of joy to sociologists, observers of customs, narrators, and film directors.

Raymond Cartier has written that there are fifty Americas, one for every State of the Union. And it's true. The people are like chameleons. At every hour of the day they change skin and color and show themselves in different styles and fashions."

Guido Gerosa

It is not possible to give a single definition to the American style and way of life. One can speak generically of a style of life without presuming to include all aspects of the same. The United States contains an infinite variety of ethnic groups, each characterized by different histories, sentiments, and temperaments. The one thing they all have in common is a deep love for that country which unites and represents them.

96-97 One of the images which most often springs to mind when speaking of the United States and its people is that of the cowboy: those skilful herdsmen who live in direct contact with nature, far from the compromises and the intrigues of business and the chaotic traffic of the large cities.

98-99 There are many different competitions in a rodeo, and they are all spectacular. The cowboys skilfully ride bareback or tame wild horses in a short time. They also wrestle with steers and compete in capturing calves using a lasso.

America
at Work

100-101 *Agriculture represents one of the principal sources of income for the American economy and ranges from the cotton fields of Louisiana and the vineyards of California to the endless wheat fields of Iowa.*

102-103 *The crayfish is a fundamental element in the local cuisine of the State of Mississippi, and the crayfish fishing industry flourishes there. In all parts of the U.S.A., fishing is practised and is a relevant source of profit.*

Lazy like a summer in Los Angeles but frenzied like Wall Street, America offers both of its faces to those who wish to get to know it. The fable of Uncle Scrooge McDuck, who created his fortune starting off with a nickel, has been surpassed today. There remains the capitalistic taste for accumulating and increasing economic well-being and the force of a professionalism reached by dint of hard work.

104-105 Wall Street is America's economic temple. It is here that the fortunes of the country are created and consolidated, and it is here that the strings of the world are pulled.

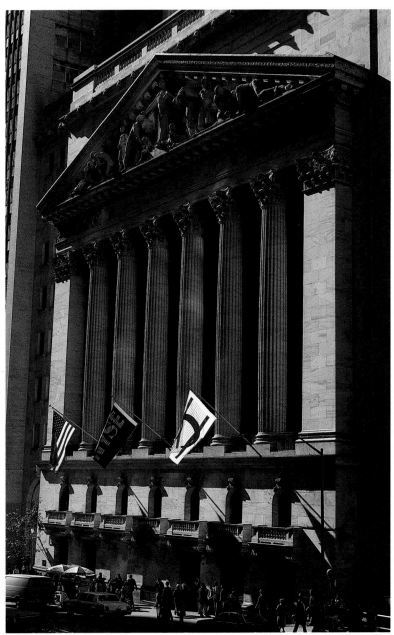

A Nation for Sport

Sport is the principal source of amusement, hobby, and pleasure relaxation in the United States. Millions of fans watch and practice a wide range of sports with great passion. Many of them also play, at an amateur level, those same sports which they admire in the large stadiums.

106-107 *The stadiums in which American football is played are often enormous, to cope with the huge crowds who follow this sport. The Superdome in New Orleans is the largest covered stadium in the world with a capacity of 97,000.*

107 left *American football players take to the field wearing light suits of "armor" which are necessary because of the violence of the game.*

107 right *Basketball also has many fans, not only because of the overpowering superiority of American teams in international competitions, but also because children play it in schools from a very early age.*

108-109 *Baseball is the quintessential American sport. Its origin dates back to the initiative of Alexander Cartwright in the last century, but the definitive rules were not laid down until 1859. The picture shows the Los Angeles stadium, in which the Dodgers have excited millions of spectators with their exploits.*

109 top *The oldest hippodrome in the U.S.A., the Saratoga Race Track, has become part of the myth of American society in the same way as Wimbledon is a legend for the United Kingdom. During the racing season, this small city comes to life and becomes the place where the exponents of high society must be seen.*

109 bottom *Golf is a very popular sport in America, and there are many excellent courses with a very high technical level.*

109

110 Sailing is the most practised sports in coastal regions. In this picture a sailboat approaches the Golden Gate Bridge at San Francisco.

110-111 In the United States all sports are loved and followed in a more or less intense manner, and occasions for creating and watching spectacles are always welcome. This photograph shows a large gathering of hot-air balloonists in Albuquerque, New Mexico.

The Art of Living

To say that entertainment was born in the United States is certainly excessive, but to claim that the Americans know how to enjoy themselves more than any other people is certainly not an exaggeration. The wide open spaces and the extraordinary natural beauty represent a remarkable starting point, but this would all be worth nothing without the spirit, enthusiasm, and organizational ability of which the inhabitants of the United States constantly give proof. A family holiday in a camper, the magic of Disneyland, an improvised show at Ghirardelli Square in San Francisco, or an important date in Hollywood, everything, really everything in America is a unique occasion not to be missed and to be lived to the fullest.

112 *An American family enjoys the sunset on a splendid beach in Florida.*

113 *The camper is the vehicle which is most commonly used to take the family on holiday, and perhaps, as in this case, to search for the most charming corners of Florida.*

114-115 *Daytona Beach, Florida is thronged with people year round because of the mildness of the climate.*

Palm Beach owes its birth and development to Henry Flagler, a rich railroad magnate and business partner of the Rockefeller family, who realized the potential of this area as a residential center in 1893 and convinced some of the best known families in the country to move to the south. Within a short time Palm Beach became the preferred residence for members of the high society, and it then developed inexorably. Today North Avenue, with its refined boutiques offering the most exclusive creations of international designers, is considered the most opulent street in the eastern United States.

118-119 If Palm Beach offers a pleasant climate and crystalline water for a serene old age, the natural calm of Georgia proposes a valid alternative for those who wish to enjoy moments of authentic tranquility.

A human jukebox along the streets of San Francisco, a tightrope walker who performs at sunset on the pier at Key West, and students playing music in the main square at Berkley University are all different aspects of a unique way of living and searching for spectacle in daily life. In the United States every spot, square, or crossroad is the ideal place for putting oneself on show, certain that one will manage to attract an attentive and well-disposed audience. America is really the world of spectacle, but at the base of this singular characteristic there is a deep respect for the individual and of his right to express himself even in non-conventional ways, as long as it is not offensive to the dignity of others.

121

122-123 *Disneyland is in Anaheim, California, 27 miles from Los Angeles on the west coast, and Disneyworld is in Orlando, Florida on the other coast of the United States. Disneyland was created by Walter Elias Disney in 1955, responding to the secret expectations of millions of children and adults. Disneyworld was its continuation 15 years later, enriched quite rightly with a better and more modern concept of an amusement park.*

124-125 *Despite the fact that the epoch in which Hollywood was famous all over the world has long gone, every tourist who visits Los Angeles tries to visit the sidewalk on which the stars have left their handprints and buys a ticket for Mann's Chinese Theater. Here one can relive the atmosphere of the great cinemas of the 1940s, which, with their bas-reliefs, stuccoes, and brocade stage curtains, were temples for the magical rites of showing films that provided the dreamstuff for entire generations.*

The Pioneers of Space

There are three space centers in the United States. The least known is in Alabama, and the more famous ones are the Lyndon B. Johnson Center at Houston, Texas, and the John F. Kennedy Center in Florida, formerly known as Cape Canaveral. Splendid American organization has made it possible for all those curious about space travel to visit the launching pads in all three centers. It is also possible to see perfect reproductions of the Apollo lunar modules as well as to try out mission simulations such as those in which the astronauts train for future missions. This work of promoting space activity has the aim of making the entire nation share in the great progress and the conquests which have been made in this sector, which presents itself as a new frontier, a challenge to the innate pioneering spirit of the Americans.

126 top left *Sophisticated instruments are capable of controlling, from earth, the missions in space.*

126 top right *The shuttle taking off from the launching pad is a spectacle of true technological power.*

126 bottom *Vaguely disturbing technological advances are at the base of progress and space conquest.*

127 *The lunar adventure is now history in the United States. Aeronautical engineering has enabled the achievement of goals which until a few years ago seemed inconceivable.*

128 *American flags outside a bar in Key West, Florida.*